A Children's Book About

BEING A BAD SPORT

Managing Editor: Ellen Klarberg
Copy Editor: Annette Gooch
Editorial Assistant: Lana Eberhard
Art Director: Jennifer Wiezel
Production Artist: Gail Miller
Illustration Designer: Bartholomew
Inking Artist: Susie Hornig
Coloring Artist: Susie Hornig
Lettering Artist: Linda Hanney
Typographer: Communication Graphics

Printed in 1991

A Children's Book About

BEING A BAD SPORT

By Joy Berry

GROLIER ENTERPRISES CORP.

This book is about Lennie.

Reading about Lennie can help you understand and deal with **being a bad sport.**

People who do not win and lose graciously
are bad sports.

Bad sports are happy only when they win.
When bad sports lose, they often:

- pout,
- cry, or
- throw tantrums.

Bad sports sometimes lie so they can win.

Bad sports sometimes cheat so they can win.

Bad sports sometimes criticize other people so they can win.

They try to make the people they criticize feel bad about themselves and lose.

Bad sports are not good winners.

They act as if they are better than the people who lose.

When bad sports win, they say and do things to make the people who lose feel bad.

Avoid being a bad sport. Try to be a good
sport instead.

Good sports realize that no one can win all the time.

They know that every person wins sometimes and loses sometimes.

They also realize that losing does not make you a bad person and winning does not make you a good person.

Good sports lose graciously. Even though they might not like to lose, they congratulate the winners.

When good sports lose, they allow the winners to enjoy winning. Good sports try to make the winners feel that they did well and deserved to win.

When good sports win, they try to help the people who lose feel good.

When good sports win, they are kind to the people who lose. Good sports encourage the people who lose to try again.

It is important to treat other people the way you want to be treated.

If you want other people to be good sports, you must be a good sport.